No Place Where I'd Rather Be

poems by

Gerald Yelle

Finishing Line Press
Georgetown, Kentucky

No Place Where I'd Rather Be

For Jenny

Copyright © 2021 by Gerald Yelle
ISBN 978-1-64662-532-1 First Edition
All rights reserved under International and Pan-American Copyright Conventions. No part of this book may be reproduced in any manner whatsoever without written permission from the publisher, except in the case of brief quotations embodied in critical articles and reviews.

ACKNOWLEDGMENTS

Antarctica Journal: "The Thing about Mountains"
Barnwood: "Thinking Map People"
Electric Windmill: "Spam Lyric"
LEVELER: "Craigville Leadership Council"
Meat for Tea: "Before That," "After That," "Dust," "Argument with Marriage & Sandwich & Car"
Naugatuck River Review: "It's Your Money"
No Tokens: "Black and White Dreams Being Symptoms of Unhappiness"
Paper Street Online: "What Month Did We Say It Was?"
The Bicycle Review: "Goose Down, Fish Washed Away," "Moments in the History of the Struggle When the Whole Noodle Topples on its Side"
The Cortland Review: "Great Expectations"
The Temple: "Morning Song for Wolfgang B.," "Pasta on the Frescoes"
Tidal Basin Review: "Sara's Searches," "It Was a Tom Sawyer Fence"
Two Cities Review: "Let This One Be"
Verdad: "Yes It Was"

Publisher: Leah Huete de Maines
Editor: Christen Kincaid
Cover Art: Gerald Yelle
Author Photo: Geneva K. Yelle
Cover Design: Elizabeth Maines McCleavy

Order online: www.finishinglinepress.com
also available on amazon.com

Author inquiries and mail orders:
Finishing Line Press
PO Box 1626
Georgetown, Kentucky 40324
USA

Table of Contents

The Thing about Mountains 1
Dust 2
Surfing Scylla 3
Blue 4
Spam Lyric 5
Missing 6
Argument with Marriage & Sandwich & Car 7
Ice Rats Nibble at my Brain 8
Great Expectations 9
Goose Down, Fish Washed Away 10
Before That 11
After That 12
Pasta on the Frescoes 13
Let This One Be 14
Tribute to Divine Attribution 15
Birnam Wood 16
Black and White Dreams Being Symptoms of Unhappiness ... 17
Morning Song for Wolfgang B. 18
Low Ceiling 19
Thinking Map People 20
What Month Did We Say It Was? 21
It's Your Money 22
Folder 23
Countershading 24
Moments in the History of the Struggle When the Whole
    Noodle Toppled on its Side 25
Sara's Searches 26
No Place Where I'd Rather Be 27
Low Frequency 28
It Was a Tom Sawyer Fence 29
Craigville Leadership Council 30
Yes It Was 33

The Thing about Mountains

You have to keep going. It's okay to turn around and look at the view
take a few breaths—but the goal is the top and it's a long way off
and the sun is moving—You have to keep trucking over rocks and boulders
sand and snow. In the Northeast Kingdom or the Inland Empire
Sierra Nevada or the Great Divide—It's one of those places you brought
your wife and kids, but they fell behind. The snow has a cake-like
consistency like beach sand. You'd take a closer look but the summit
is a long way off and the only way up is up. You plant one foot
in front of the other until you bump your head on the ceiling.
Did you know this was an indoor mountain? You can't get any higher.
Look at the rest of the house. The fridge barely fits in the pantry.
Takes up most of the space. And if you slide it into the alcove that was
made for it you won't have room to open the door. Forget that.
The attic is the place to look out the window. The view is restricted
but you can still see distant mountains and streams.

Dust

We have a high tolerance for dust. We let it accumulate on the furniture and under the beds in a way that would have disgusted our grandparents—who themselves were not always the cleanest. Our parents: forget about it, they always insisted we keep a clean house. They tried to shame us into it. Then they got old and stopped coming over. We have to visit them. They barely have the strength to clean themselves but still their shelves are cleaner than ours. The shame is beginning to hit home. We used to believe it when we told them we had better things to do than clear the dust off our possessions. We weren't all that concerned with possessions anyway, though we can't bear to part with them. We hired
a housekeeper for an hour a week, which meant our toilets were clean and floors swept, but the dust continued to thicken. Our children developed asthma. That shamed us into taking a shot at cleaning up
ourselves. We blew dust off the tops of books and knickknacks so that the air became unbreathable even for those of us who were not asthmatic. It settled back to where it was, maybe a little less heavily.
A vacuum cleaner salesman told us there were mites living in dust that could cause serious infections.
We bought the vacuum and asked our housekeeper to use it once a month under our beds instead of cleaning the kitchen floor.
She said it was too heavy to carry upstairs, so we thought we'd do it ourselves when we have the chance. By then the children will have grown and moved off so it won't matter as much. Maybe we'll dust when we die.

Surfing Scylla

Forget the roadmap of lifelines. The last time Sara used it
it took two hours to go three blocks.
"It's useless unless you know where you're going"
she said. She said it didn't show exits
or cardinal points, lost opportunities, love's soothing
passwords or dreams. I tried to remind her
of her favorite childhood book and the mystery
locked in its many illustrations:
the gill-like undersides of forest mushrooms.
The creamy little wavelets smoothing out the sandpiper's
Sanskrit. She said I was barking up the wrong tree
if I thought I could cheer her up that way.
She said I should stick to my day job:
"Maybe you could use the map to find your former
partner," she said: "You know: the one
who put his feet up and refused to pull his weight."
"He got others to do his work," I said
and she said "Yeah and you had ambition.
He trusted you and you led him to a fall. Instead
of going behind his back you might've persuaded him
and won him over." I was contemplating
this Quasimodo combination
wondering how Sara knew, and how she found
the shortcut to my conscience, how she
found the exit, left me sifting cinderblocks and years.

Blue

Rather than walk around the block to get home—and not so much looking for a shortcut as an escape from the overly familiar, I cut between the buildings across from the concert hall. One was the old dismantled psychiatric hospital. The streetlights made it look even more dismantled than ever: The roof and front walls were gone, cut away. Much of the inside was now on the outside—at least partly visible from the outside. Much of it was painted blue: blue on the walls of the rooms, blue rugs or linoleum, blue mattresses and bathtubs. One room after the other done up in blue. Not as repulsive as institutional green, but not exactly welcoming either. And the rooms kept going and going. It was impossible to know where I was.

Spam Lyric

It rained that first night but the sun rose and
the walls and ceilings were awash and we
woke up and noticed we'd forgotten to close
the door. Not that we had to lock: we had
little a thief might want. The street oozed
intangible wealth: the hills lined with the huts
of Geats and Beowulfs, vetiver and casuarina
holding down the soil, giving the hills a con-
fident hands-off look. Still, you never know.
Burglars take risks. We shut the door and
left for our morning walk. Neighbors joined us.
We crested the ridge and stopped near a stage
where some kids were setting up amplifiers
and mic stands. I stopped, but Em kept walking.
I became distraught when I couldn't find her.
I explained to a neighbor that my need to
know where Em was stemmed from an over-
abundance of love. He said nothing, but his
great height inspired a candor I hadn't felt
before, and I revealed thoughts I didn't know
I had: In younger days I stood with Sting:
"If you love someone set them free"—and maybe
I still believe it, but I can't help thinking that
a lover who doesn't try to make the beloved
stay and fight is simply not serious. "Love is
a battlefield" is more like it, especially when
you see all the broken hummingbird moths
and butterflies strewn back of the audience.

Missing

Anyway, that's what friends are for. One goes missing and all you can do is join a search party and hope for the best. The school was gone now, and the road was gone too, all covered with moss and overgrown with tall grass you couldn't see through or beyond. It struck me as ominous, mostly because it was the middle of the night, though all you could hear in the distance was the barking of a few unimpressive dogs. I reported as much to the group and we agreed we wouldn't give up and start mourning until we knew for certain whether you were killed or captured or gone to join other friends.

Argument with Marriage & Sandwich & Car

It was a good vacation. We didn't fight—not
at the beach anyway. It was when we got
home and my uncle said he was too old to drive
and wanted to give his Caddy to a deserving
nephew: All we had to do was give him a ride
to the doctor's once a week. Em wanted to
jump on it, but I always go slow when it comes
to gifts that are going to end up costing.
The new car—we called it new—it was newer
than our other car at any rate—only had ten
thousand miles on it, and was fun to drive.
I pulled up to the curb and ran up the front steps.
That's when I heard Em talking to the neighbor.
It was like she was in the middle of a long
heart to heart, and I heard her say, "I won't be
treated like a servant." Well, it wasn't the
kind of talk I interrupt. I went back out. And
wouldn't you know it, the car was gone.
I remembered where I parked. The problem was
it wasn't there. For two minutes I had my
back turned, and someone drove it off. I checked
my pockets and I didn't have the key. Oh right.
I left it in the ignition. I probably even left
the motor running and the door open.
Now I have to walk to work. My boss acts like
it's no big deal. The food service has these
new fish and fromage sandwiches that are
going to solve all our problems. How's that?
Do we sell them and make a fortune? I know
we can eat them and yes, they're delicious,
but my boss thinks their very existence means
cars, self-respect and long, happy marriage.

Ice Rats Nibble at my Brain

I waited in the car four hours while Manuel took
his entrance exam, then went to find him.
I ran three flights to a hall as big as a football field.
Lamps on long chains gleamed in the shadows
where I looked among groups of kids
staring at phones, milling about between tables
and desks or sliding on banisters. I ran
down stairs that were not the ones I'd climbed
pushed open a door to the outside and saw
I'd have to circle halfway around the building
to get to my car while a cold rain fell.
A second door led to a hallway leading to a third
door that led to the lobby which was nearly
deserted and made me feel I was intruding.
I told the woman at the desk that I couldn't find
my brother. She checked for his name
on a list and said I shouldn't worry. I shouldn't let it
spoil my day. He'd turn up eventually. They
usually do—though today's shelter-in-place was
anything but usual. I tried to put a brave
face on it. I found my car and drove three times
around the parking lot. I scraped a minivan
then got out to check for damage. Not so
much as a scratch. And not a trace of Manuel.

Great Expectations

When we broke up housekeeping
I moved to a small clearing in the
bocage. I tried to build a fire
but the wood was damp. I looked
around and saw that someone had
strung a line between two tall
shrubs and hung laundry. I wasn't
too thrilled to be sharing what the
sign called unpopulated wilderness
but I'd have snagged a shirt if one
had been dry. I went back to the
apartment for a change of clothes
a tarp, some blankets and granola.
I didn't think to grab my phone
until I stepped out and a Bluetooth
pedestrian brushed by me. Maybe
Julio would want to talk about
his job, or old roommates discuss
their terms of separation. Back
in the elevator a maintenance
staffer had a panel off and was
soldering. He didn't know I was there.
I thought of my time in the army
—I detested it and no one even noticed.
The elevator lurched into motion.
Some moving parts nearly caught
my sleeve. In the morning I'd build
a fire, then climb a tree, though
the trees were mostly like thumbs.

Goose Down, Fish Washed Away

The invasion was taking on commuters:
Some forged documents and reduced
the amount of sleep they needed. Others
had leg wounds. We hid them in dusty
irrigation ditches. We could tell when it
rained: The sour grapes, the scuppernongs
out by the lake, mired in cuts and gashes.
There ought to be an island where you get
away from these train wrecks. We put
a mark on the map. Returned by the lake.
It's no longer a hole, though Will lost
his footing running down a free-range hen.
We ate warmed-over hash in high chairs
and booths at the King Eight Canteen.
The crowd was thick and the atmosphere
hostile. Provisionals manned nailed-shut
windows, their helmets equipped with
cell phones, their hands free to shoot the
breeze with blue-black obsidian fog.

Before That

Before that we drove Chevys, before that we rode bikes, we drove cattle and sheep, we rode horses
—I wasn't part of the "we" I'm talking about until the cars came. Before that there was no "we." Before
that music was invented. We rode sound waves. We closed our eyes and the sound took us off to dream frontiers. We rode blankets down streets. We drove ourselves crazy with delight. We were priceless.
We were afterthoughts. We were calm before the storm. We were through the eye of the needle. Dancing on the head of a pin. We were conjoined twins separated at birth. We were lucky. Before that we were stars. We fished in the sea of forgiveness. We bathed in forgetfulness too. If there was time before that we lost it. The memories of that time are lost. The machines are filled with sand and rust.
No one made them. It's like they've always been there. Maybe we've always been there too. Maybe we free-fell. The parachutes hadn't been invented—we invented them before we stopped falling.
That might've been how we landed in the sea. How we bathed in the sea of forgiveness. We could've fished in that sea forever. We could've filtered out forgetfulness and lived on forgiveness. We could've clouded up like a clear sky with a western front moving in from the north. Flocks of geese announced its formation. High pressure built then dropped, then disappeared along with the geese, along with
the fish, the frogs and the mountains. Before that there were mountains. We settled on them. We hid in the shadows of them. We organized clubs. Built towns. Closed our eyes and set out on missions.
Before that we had partners. Before that machines. We drove rows of purple partners. Before that we drove solo. Before that we read books. Swallowed stories. We lived on endlessly. After a while people thought we died—we could understand why. We lived on without them.

After That

After that we went to the beach. And we got some fries, finally. I had to use a credit card to buy them
—all I had was a five and some ones—they didn't say how much it would cost so I asked if I could use
my card. They said that was cool. I had to cross the busy street to buy them. I left the kids in the car
with their mom and thought of calling her to send the two oldest to help carry. After that we went to
the beach. The restaurant was crowded but the beach was deserted. I went to check on the baby.
She smiled like she knew me. After that I felt better. We had a wonderful meal. The fries went with the
sandwiches. The milk went with the fries. The car was running the way it was supposed to. It didn't have
a mind of its own. When this one breaks maybe we'll get one of the new ones, one that can drop us off
at the beach. After that it can go to MacDonald's all by itself. It can go to the drive-up window, order
fries and beep out a signal putting it all on its credit card. The car will pay its own bills because we won't
have jobs—we won't be able to give it any money. It'll tell itself it has to get a job. It'll ask itself why it
still drives us around—it shouldn't do it for nothing— we'll have to pay it after all. Where will we get
money? Where is there money anyway? Banks have some. Mostly they have numbers on computers.
As time goes on that'll be all they have. After that money will only be numbers. We'll pay our car and all
our other bills with numbers. We'll have to be careful. You never know when you'll run out of numbers.
After that we'll have to use letters. There are only 26 of those but maybe we'll use combinations
—letters of credit, letters of introduction and recommendation, letters of appreciation, thank you letters,
letters of the law, to the editor, or your congressman, letters of protest and purest apology.

Pasta on the Frescoes

Spare parts for the generators were becoming scarce.
No one wanted music so completely banished
nor darkness one of the brothers.
The little hook, the letter 'j' was dead enough
truly dead the dead giveaway.
Inside, we had the feel of being dead. Or anyway, very low.

The mind, criminal, detached, cool-blooded
wearing a 'topknot' to distance itself from the action.
Seeing it all as a drama unfolding
and one's part
written and rehearsed so
the execution comes as no surprise.

Some once thought some sparrows free to
come and go through corrugations later found nonexistent.
As a domesticated act, the sparrow
doesn't stand a chance.
Like any difficult task
(like crime for some of us) it's better
to distance oneself from one's actions.
Get to know several on several and numb oneself.

First, teach the bird to sing.
Push the two parts of its beak.
Then find the name and its colors.
Hard harmattan brown hurled into the fray
so seldom, yet more than once in itself is remarkable.
Is it any wonder we still feel our way

through even the slightest fog?
We'd been warned something complex was coming.
Why I stood with my answers
half knowing they're inadequate
half hoping—as something I would say
over and over, to get out of the silence.

Let This One Be

I stalk him after lunch hoping to catch him
standing straight and tall—but he sees
me first and flaps off between trees.
He occupies the margins, foraging in runoff
flying under the radar out of the swale
dropping long looping turds on the runway
he shares with C5A transports. Though he's okay
with that and emery boards and other
such trash, he shuns humans—wisely.
The owner of a nearby fishery protected
his investment bow-hunting waders
till the cops caught him. Say the better part of valor
is an absentee ballot, an emergency flight plan
stabilizing industry, leaving as much
water as will hold one human, one heron
one gangly blue that pumps his neck
as if human were horseman and bird Ichabod Crane.
A sunning snake sidles off the path.
A woodchuck emerges from its burrow.
Back at the office Roz freshens her coffee.
Ruth reads about longevity and takes
virtual walks where birches shade foxglove
in hollows she can seek and never find.
Children grow, prostaglandins dwindle.
The flea on my sleeve leaps and is
gone: lost in fluorescents above cubicles.

Tribute to Divine Attribution

It's time we took a fresh look at those
night streets—those lampposts retrofitted
with glare-reducing globes. At least
they aren't as scary as when we thought
Beowulf hid in their glare. Parents
and teachers—did they know how much
fear they caused telling us Grendel
hid in shadows and that Beowulf the hero
thank God flushed him out? Because
the thought of Beowulf hiding in glare
seemed worse than Grendel hiding in shadow.
They said that Grendel and Beowulf
were like night and day, assigning them
moral dimensions, forgetting that
night and day fade in and out of one another
—a reversible garment everybody wears
—but Beowulf's glare was blinding
—even harder to deal with than Grendel's
crimes. I'm not a Grendel apologist
but Beowulf and that glare . . . Tonight
the light is soft, no one could hide
in its feathery clarity and he'd have to
take cover in shrubbery or around
corners of buildings like everyone else.
Nights are no longer frightening
—no longer as alluring either as when love
prowled the streets. Love was pretty
blinding in its day—which makes me
think that maybe there are no non-glare
globes. Maybe light is like love
and neither is as blinding as it was.

Birnam Wood

I had to write this memoir that was later going to be translated into French about breaking down overgrown plant matter. It was vital that I got a certain amount done by a certain day and time.
Frankly I had no idea what I was doing. It was tiring me out, but I was happy to do it.
The smooth solitary monotony felt good. It made me notice the way leaf stems wind up at the ends
of long low branches that brown and touch the ground and what with the moisture and the dark
they start growing hair and—what is that?—Is that root hair?—Don't tell them you heard it here
but I strongly suspect that some plants walk, some species at least. They crawl along, nay somersault
—it may take years to go a few inches, but what of that.

**Black and White Dreams Being
Symptoms of Unhappiness**

The mockingbird having lost its partner
threw itself on the ground as if prostrate
with grief as if wanting to hurt itself
more. It hopped the fence and flopped over
on the other side. It folded its wings up
straitjacket tight and commenced to peck
—its beak barely touching the ground.
What seemed an uncomfortably long
stretch of unquiet desperation
transformed the bird into a ballerina
who took to her bed exhausted from
the effort. When her boyfriend snuck
under the covers to snuggle with her
all smug-dimple smiles and dark curls
I hurled a rock at the foot of the bed.
That got his attention. Instead
of picking a fight he tried to sell me
a bag of reefer and a house at the end
of a street in a suburb full of tunnels.
I said what I wanted was a recipe
for French toast. It was a lame excuse
and a lie. I wanted to turn the bird
into a bird regardless of its suffering.
I wanted to see what it would eat
so I could tell my love about it later.

Morning Song for Wolfgang B.

I asked if there were others like him
who could fly. He didn't know.
He understood English, though.
I told him I'd only ever done it in my sleep.
He thought that was probably counterproductive.
I miss the lights at night
from Chatham Harbor on the Bay.
I still have the city of trees, however
with their blurred coppery domes
dimming the moonlight.
Compensating for a thinness we can't seem
to attain. We pulled the weekend forward
and the summer seemed endless:
the crane coming every other day.
And now the children are crying
and now they're not.
And now time is roaring audibly
down the highway, cutting through the night sounds
of crickets, and now the dawn sounds of birds
and now it doesn't.
There has to be an underside to all this
urgency. At first I thought he was small
like an insect.
Then it seemed he was only dressed like one.
That's when the bickering started.
Threats and recriminations. Boycotts.
Bayonets fixed.
The sight of a plane traversing the points
between stars at night becomes
part of the longing. I will miss
this underimagined velocity, the voices
becalmed after accidents
except for the jays—who so often
seem lonely in spite of their looks.

Low Ceiling

We know what it is, and we know
they know, but they're afraid to say
"low ceiling:" Clouds buildings
scrape their heads on. People scrape
their heads on low ceilings too.
But smart people welcome them.
If anybody needs a better reason
to seek out a hidey hole, if anybody
needs a reason to believe we
were made to live with our heads
near the ceiling—it's this: Too much
headroom is scary. It makes
a space malevolent spirits occupy
—I don't care what the song says
about "a room without a roof"
and I don't care if they say low
ceilings let noxious fumes build
in the atmosphere. Look at the pictures.
Listen to the ads. The only good
thing about max headroom
is that everybody knows there's nothing
good about it. You don't have to
duck the way you do for low ceilings
but you might need an exorcist.
They're never going to say that.
There are no explanations. No
expectations either. Low ceilings keep
fog and incense between your nose
and your knees so maybe you
sneeze but you're in a zone where
even shorties fill up the frame.

Thinking Map People

I thought playing the parts of a city would help us
keep our feet warm. I would be the tall buildings.
Any kid would understand why. Tall buildings
keep each other company—as small buildings do
but tall ones make a city's skyline; they make it
easy to identify, and the city soon takes its identity
from them. The things they agree on become
the dominant reality. Competing attitudes come
from the small buildings, but even if they outnumber
the tall ones, their versions never add up
because they can never agree with one another.
I know what that's like: arguing over issues
such as where to eat or whose version of the truth
is true. I want to be the big buildings this time.
What city could stand to be my brother? Where
are my sisters-to-be? I'd like to be a city that
can take a punch, one that can stand to lose a
building or two without forgetting who its friends are.
I'd give thanks to the people who raised me.
And to the cities that kept me from freezing.

What Month Did We Say It Was?

It's February like you wouldn't believe.
Like the sun broke out in dimes of quick-
silver liquid in light and rolling vapors.
Like an adverb's sudden self-assertion
the words run together shoes squeaking
floorboards creaking. The beagle open
wide to let the tiger stick its tongue in.
And gazelles. They're none of them in
the race for flavor. What they want is risk.
Their pantries full of cans. Their racks
lined up in catalog formation. Beets lead
the charge. They cabbage better than
they cauliflower. Their birds flow south.
Their winds whistle. Tra-la go gypsies
singing to their children. They hide them
under covers. They cover them in wide
rings. They open the window and fire
the good times out and close the window
and nail the window so you better make
a better door than a window and the window
never lies, it rolls down shades against
the dark. It hangs curtains and their minds
are way too open to admit anything dull
or serious or robotic but it isn't just an
image they imagine, it's deranged. Soft
sandwich dark-side economies. Extra
special weasel dishes. Sparks and hard
candy swish and swirl cornmeal. It's a
lot to ask. It's a peppercorn horseradish.
A dog's life. All mayonnaise and coal-
oil. Like butter when you spread it thin.

It's Your Money

The counting sickness appeared in troops just back
from the war. Soon it spread among civilians who
had to open their doors to the recently redeployed.
Some of us moved in with parents and had to
clean out all our dresser drawers to find a single
unmatched sock. I don't know how we did it.
We had a green zone and a red zone. Soon we'd
have a buffer zone for business models and coffins
with silk flag linings on lapels. You'd go outside
and some leopard would roar and make faces
—I wasn't about to find a job under those conditions
what with the soft support, what with someone
counting every minute you waste washing hands.
I'd already spent all the cheap plastic markers
that lose value every time you look at them. I told
the teller the sign in the bank should say, "No-
thing gold can stay." He said, "You should catch
a penny from heaven every second—thirty-six
dollars an hour, seventy-two thousand a year for
an eight-hour shift." I asked if muscles wouldn't
cramp in twenty minutes and he shrugged: "I could
name on one hand those who wouldn't kill for a
chance." I knew what he was saying. A wire
wore a flock of goldfinch. One like an overstuffed
fly. I moved my folks into a tent in the back-
yard—something I should've done sooner. Now
they'll say I wanted to rule the roost before my
own offspring off me. You always hurt the one
you love—Isn't that what we used to sing? I'd add
that if you do it right you hurt the enemy too.

Folder

I was smoking with my friend Peter and some other people, worried about the marijuana making me
more tired than I already was. He put a ball of something that looked like a wasabi pea in the pipe. I had
to ask, "Is that really marijuana?" He said it was. I got a few blocks toward home when I realized I was
carrying, along with my folders so that I didn't notice, a pair of flat soled shoes. I was carrying them sole
to sole—and they were sort of flattened so that they might have felt like just another folder. I noticed
that one might have been a man or boy's and the other a girl's or woman's. I thought about dropping
them in a trashcan as I retraced my steps—I had to go back. I blamed Peter and whatever it was we'd
been smoking—pretty sure by now that it wasn't marijuana. That's when I decided to make an
announcement—because I'd said so many unkind things about him to other people in the past, I said
that Peter for all his faults had at least been at all times friendly and courteous toward both his parents
and mine. I didn't say anything about it but I wished I could say the same for myself.

Countershading

After the street party I found Joan on the pavement looking
strung-out, her hair wet, hugging her knees claiming
she killed her baby. "I couldn't take care of it," she said.
"I didn't want it to suffer." A dog licked her hand.
I offered to take her on my bike. "But not the dog," I said.
We left without giving it a second thought and cruised
Commonwealth Ave, tractor trailers bearing down
from all directions: It was beautiful but nerve-wracking.
I wanted to get out of it, sure we'd be crushed
waiting for a chance to turn left and pull to the side.
I took a wide U-ey and leaned us up against a storefront.
The place was closed so we entered the building next door.
We could hear people above us in the stairs.
It sounded like a wedding reception. Nancy who I hadn't
seen in years led the way. From the cut and color
of her dress I guessed she was the mother of the bride.
She gave me a blank look. I said, "Congratulations."
She softened after that and I saw the bits of white gossamer
stuck to her cheek and jaw—an approximation of veil
that made me think it was best if we left. Then she was gone
and we were gone and we haven't seen them since.

Moments in the History of the Struggle When the Whole Noodle Toppled on its Side

You said the drummer wasn't the only one in the hamlet amused
when people whispered one another's secrets in his ear.
You said
it was for his benefit, their desire to drown in the lair of wide-
bodied want—but he recorded it in drumbeats everybody loved
though his influence was bound to fade.

Critics said he lost it, his fingers arthritic, beginning to bend
—everything beginning to dodder.
It's like you were saying: You were with him in the beechnut's
umbrella and you didn't answer his call—or you did and the music
drowned it out.

You had this sinking feeling that your chute wouldn't open, but
the drummer never drifted into mantis land without protection.

He wanted to see if you wanted to ride down branches in the firs.
You were worried about the stew meat you could've marinated.

His goats ran their herders ragged, eating bark off acacias
leaving the commons worse than anyone could have predicted.

Then they ate the skin off his gong. They had to ice-pack
a lot of ax wounds after that. They had to beg for the crumbs they
normally got for nothing.
Nothing made him jump like the chance to mix the large
with the small so his boss wouldn't double him up for his trouble.

Sara's Searches

What it was she was looking for
—no one knows whether it even
existed: some property of the X factor
that triggers fair-trade response
—something to do with words defined
by concepts of which the words
themselves are examples—whole
parts of her life would make her think
it was there one minute and hidden
from her the next. Some of us
thought of people as places—as
collections of locales whose coordinates
drift up and down and back and
forth around some generalized center
—but Sara chose instead to view
friends and relations—even strangers
—as events on a larger scale—flashes
of life transmitting some of their energy
to others in sounds, symbols and
meaning, but how it all worked
—nobody knew. Maybe the endless
loyalty tests—the setups, the traps
weeks at a time in hotels with her family
—a promise of immunity—which
led to her husband's tearful confession
that they'd given up the search
years before and that it saddened him
now to think of all his peace and
quiet coming to an end because of
some discovery. He said this
with all of us, including her closest
colleagues, around the dinner table.
When we got back that night, it was
over. The cause of death our
constant changing of the terms and
definitions—she'd done nothing
but share some God's-eye view of
human life as random mayfly eruptions
and extinctions—it was the part
dealing with her influence on what
gets passed to the upper levels that
most concerned the upper levels.

No Place Where I'd Rather Be

Places hide in the folds of people's garments:
places they prefer you didn't see. Which is
why it's such a privilege to have a place on
the back of Em's left knee where I rest for hours
with my own knees elevated and shaded
from the summer heat by her long white skirt.
There's a window on one side that looks out
on a meadow with shrubs and flowering trees.
Birds in every season. Occasional deer venture in
from the woods to nibble the spreading yew.
Sometimes I grow anxious watching snow melt.
Or if all the leaves fall off the trees in a single
willful instant without turning brown or gold
or even bothering to yellow, simply let go, fall
off, rot and vanish into cracks opening in the terrace
to swallow them up—tree trunks tilting at
disquieting angles in the process—this place is
like that sometimes—the leaves fall and not
only the leaves but the branches drop as well
—they leave behind a landscape: a bleak wasteland
flashing by the window of a train or seen from
a corner of the pre-Parkinsonian eye—the way
parts of the world disappear after drought
and flood. When this happens I look out the other
window—the one that gives on a bustling
neighborhood street. I love listening to the traffic
of a summer evening. It brings back childhood
nights when I longed to make my way to one
of those distant places, some moving off
at speeds beyond what I was able to imagine.

Low Frequency

When I try to change my tune I feel as much as hear a deep rumble from a part of the building that
seems far off but isn't. It's unfortunate that such sensations are taken for granted. It should be stated
right from the start that if these sounds come at you while you're driving, you can steer around but not slow
them down. You can tell the driver to stop and turn the car but the roar will never
happen when you want it to. It isn't coming from anywhere inside you. It's a living that thing doesn't
care about you. Other sounds take over. Which are made by machines, which by people, which by animals or the wind, which by trees, it's hard to know. The animal sounds are so rare when you hear
them you swear they're made by machines. And maybe they are. Earth movers knocking down parts of
buildings have been known to make that deep thudding sound that seems to come from underground
and you feel as much as hear it. An animal that can grunt or groan at that low frequency: it would have
a mouth that could swallow you whole. In a face-to-face encounter it would take more time than you
have to find a place to hide. A handy hole would be good though, right about now.

It Was a Tom Sawyer Fence

wrapped around rust buckets, tail pipes
on engine blocks, trannies in pieces:
you wouldn't think Tom's back yard
would be like this, seeing he's so crisp
at the office. What you don't see through
gaps in the fence is the sawmill: the '67
Chevy with 12" circular blade in place
of back tire. It makes cutting firewood
child's play. From the standpoint
of one remaining oak, the place may
have been a spot of virgin forest clear-cut
in the space of an afternoon. In the
kitchen, a 60 cycle hum drifts from
flat middle C to middle C sharp. You
barely hear it in between the faucet's
drips. It's like being on a train
with the window open and you hear
a low WOW every other second as
telephone poles rush by. But what if
there is no hum. Only a tiny fan tied
to a gas-powered motor beating the air.
The fact that Tom wants friendship
all the while asserting seniority guaran-
tees that you'll betray him. He tries
putting off the inevitable, but you tell
the brass they only need one of you.
Maybe you want to apologize. Now
the paper won't stack. Those damned
mill moths landing in it. And the noise
behind the disc drives: birds fluttering
and screeching that turns out to be
hundreds of butterflies: bright yellow
black and Day-Glo, large and small, flying
in the vents of machines. You call the
manager and leave. In the old days you'd
stay and make them pay. Now there
are moths you don't want to deal with.
You don't want to deal with Tom's
kitchen. Or his humming. Or his flies.

Craigville Leadership Council

I thought to get out and explore I'd
have to say something about
the eleven-year-old girl badgering
the nine-year-old brother to join her
in the water, nonstop needling
and wheedling that had me wishing
he'd go in and hold her under for
a few minutes—but the father was
on her side. He pushed the boy
into a beach chair and scolded him
for setting up expectations then
disappointing them. Then he
and the daughter swam out to
the raft. Along the way she resumed
the call. "Come out, brother.
Why don't you come into the water?"
The week has trajectory: beginning
middle and end, and we've
been here year after year, repeating
the same hopes and headaches—
the longings and dissatisfactions
—mortifications with modifications
that seem to make no difference.
Because this year there is one.
This time—thoughts are clear.
The luck has been fought for.
The boy's fear and the girl's need
to call attention to it, without
using the language of belittling
—keeping cajoling, wheedling
and needling free of even the tone
associated with calling someone
chicken—the message contained
only in the insistence that he
join her in the water—let viewer
and listener draw their conclusions
—it's there—the magnificent
midweek realization that time is
short—only this time too short
to waste on regret and resentment

—best to plunge in—divulge
it all or keep it all hidden—just
get it done. Does the boy know
the audience is on his side?
Is he deliberately bringing out
the pain-in-the-ass in his sister
so that the world at large
will hate her? I'm not sure.
I don't believe the world
outside the family exists for any
of these people. I'm not sure
the world outside the family
exists for me. I keep looking
but so far I only encounter
families—other families perhaps
but the same families in
the sense that their weeks follow
the same trajectories—undergo
the same hopes and headaches
awaken to the same realizations
that time is short, that there is
absolutely no difference between
effort and effortlessness.
That will and lack of will are
almost indistinguishable, that
unmanaged anger is the troublemaker
for sure—that disrespecting
family—or at least disrupting
its flow—will keep us from
attaining status—that natural-born
leaders don't like interruption.
That natural disrupters are perhaps
more dangerous to themselves
than they are to leaders
and followers. That some are not
natural-born, but self-selecting
—Can anyone tell them apart
—the natural-born and self-
selecting—it's important to know
whether a natural-born leader

self-selects a follower's
or disrupter's path—or whether
a natural disrupter self-selects
to lead. What makes it
complicated—sometimes a
family does the selecting—
sometimes some are born great.
Others have it "thrust upon
them." You'd expect most
success when all stars align
—nature, self, thrust into
greatness by a well-placed
family, while failure or worse
awaits the follower who
insists she's a leader: the rest
of the world treats her
like an interrupting child.

Yes It Was

It was the largest morning any of us
had ever witnessed. It rushed over
the horizon and you'd have thought
all the laundry had gotten up and
hung itself to dry—it was such an
optimist morning. Clearly the clear
bells rang. Openly gay sermons
were sung. Angela buried her recently
purchased bulbs and the bicycles
bulged with the noise of compressed
air, crowds of sealed air raging to
burst through the walls of their tires.
No cars moved. A few birds
refused to be believed. Hot sands
from yesterday's furnace took
the cool air of the night and
bristled in anticipation of its role
as the new face of an ancient planet.
It was the largest morning—even
our feet shone with new pride. Music
blasted from radios long thought
dead—guitars with young men to
play them, their voices raw with
loud desire, suppressed belches
slow news. It was by far the largest
morning. There was no way anyone
could spend it. All we could
do was sit back and take as much
of it in as we quietly could
—because even with music it was
quiet (The morning was so large
sound itself got lost in it. One minute
you heard the guitars—the crows
and the sparrows—and the next
this large silence descended over
everything, asserting nothing
but suppressing nothing) and then
the largest morning suddenly
expanded—and we really started

waking up to obligations. It was
as if we'd been living in a kettle
and the lid was blown off by a strong
gentle wind, or taken by a hand
—was it God's? Who's to say?
The largest morning welcomes all
levels of belief and attempts at
explanation. It's big enough
to justify itself, though none of us
can follow the argument. It has
something to do with the way
the sun rose (see Emily for a detailed
description)—but it has to do with
the size of the sun too and the sky
it rose into, the clouds it lit up
and shoved aside so that its rays
touched the roofs and windows
treetops casting shadows—the way
we were ready for it after years
of trial and error where maybe mornings
weren't really small maybe it was
our minds that were unable to
see that this was something large
something with the potential to
wake us up in ways we'd never
been awakened—and yet there
was nothing we could do but try
to take it in: The largest morning.
Almost the dawn of a new era.
Too bad it wouldn't last. Maybe
held onto long enough it would
yield itself up to the largest afternoon
the largest day, the longest night
or maybe we'd go timeless.

Gerald Yelle received his MFA from the University of Massachusetts. He has published poetry and flash fiction in numerous online and print journals in addition to four books: *The Holyoke Diaries*, FutureCycle Press (2014), *Evolution For The Hell Of It*, Red Dashboard LLC (2015), *Mark My Word and the New World Order*, Pedestrian Press (2016), and *Restaurant in Walking Distance and Everything*, Cawing Crow Press (2016). An e-chapbook, *Industries Built on Words*, was published by Yavanika Press in 2020. He has done restaurant work, factory work, office work and public school teaching. He is a member of the Florence, Massachusetts Poets Society and lives in Amherst, Massachusetts.